FLORIDA

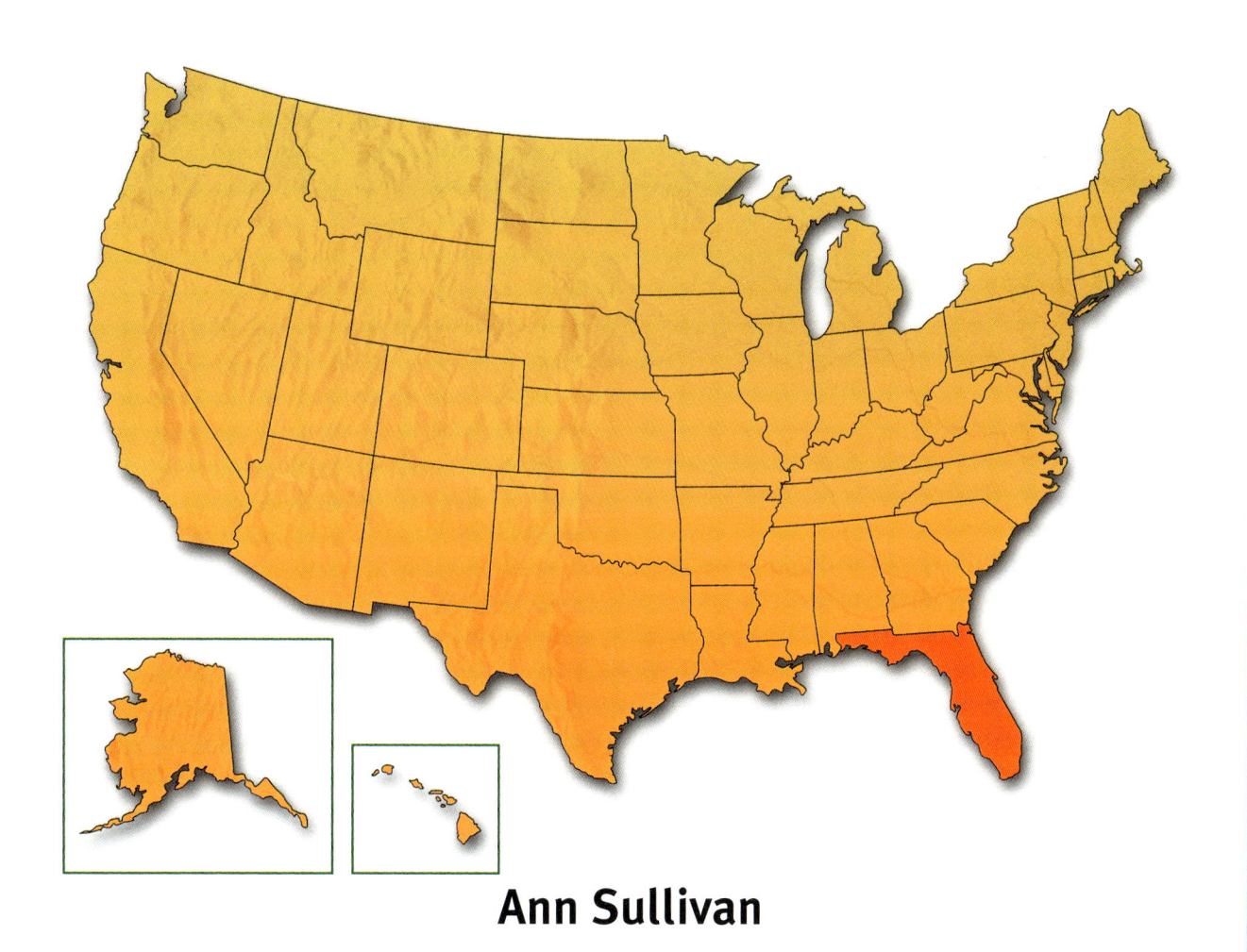

Ann Sullivan

Published by Weigl Publishers Inc.
123 South Broad Street, Box 227
Mankato, MN 56002
USA
Copyright © 2001 WEIGL PUBLISHERS INC.
All rights reserved. No part of this publication may be reproduced, stored in a retrieval system, or transmitted in any form or by any means, electronic, mechanical, photocopying, recording, or otherwise, without the prior written permission of Weigl Publishers Inc.

Library of Congress Cataloging-in-Publication Data available upon request from the publisher. Fax: (507)388-2746 for the attention of the Publishing Records Department.

ISBN 1-930954-30-1

Printed in the United States of America
1 2 3 4 5 6 7 8 9 0   05 04 03 02 01

Editor
Rennay Craats
Design
Warren Clark
Copy Editor
Heather Kissock
Cover Design
Terry Paulhus
Layout
Linda Bryksa

Photograph Credits
Every reasonable effort has been made to trace ownership and to obtain permission to reprint copyright material. The publishers would be pleased to have any errors or omissions brought to their attention so that they may be corrected in subsequent printings.

Cover: Children (Visit Florida), Oranges (Corel); **Archive Photos:** pages 3B-R, 21B-L, 24B-L, 24T-L (Santi Visalli Inc.), 24M-L (Popperfoto), 26T-L (Reuters/Jim Young), 26M-R (Reuters/Marc Serota), 26B-M (Reuters/Pierre duCharme); **Corel Corporation:** pages 3T-L, 4B-M, 7M-R, 8T-L, 8B-R, 9T-L, 10T-L, 10M-R, 10B-L, 10M-R, 11T-L,11M-R, 11B-L, 12B-L, 14T-R, 15T-R, 15T-L, 15B-R, 15B-L, 23T-L, 28T-L, 28T-R, 28B-R, 29T-R; **Cuban American Heritage Festival Society:** page 23M; **Florida State Archives:** pages 5M-L, 9B-L, 13B-R, 13T-L, 14B, 14T-L,16T-L, 16B-L, 16B-R, 17T-L, 17M-L, 17M-L, 19T-R, 19M-L, 19B-L, 21B-R, 22M-R, 23T-R, 23B-L, 24B, 29B-R; **Glenbow Archives, Calgary, Canada:** pages 18T-R (NA-1628-2), 18B-L (NA-3022-1); **Seminole Tribe of Florida:** pages 22T-L, 22B, 22M-L; **Visit Florida:** pages 3B-L, 3T-R, 3M-R, 4T-L, 4M-R, 4M-L, 4B-L, 5T-L, 5B-L, 6T-L, 6B-R, 6B-L, 7T-L, 7B-R, 8B-L, 9T, 9M-R, 12T-L, 12M-R, 12M-L, 13T-R, 13B-L, 17B-L, 20T-L, 20M-R, 20B, 21T-L, 25B-L, 25B-R, 26M-L, 27B-L, 27B-R, 28B-L, 29B-L, 29T-L; **Visuals Unlimited:** 25T-L (Jeff Greenberg), 25M-R (Charles Sanders), 27T-L (H.Q. Stevens).

CONTENTS

Introduction 4

Land and Climate 8
Natural Resources 9
Plants and Animals 10

Tourism 12
Industry 13
Goods and Services 14

First Nations 16
Explorers 17
Missionaries 18
Early Settlers 19

Population 20
Politics and Government 21
Cultural Groups 22
Arts and Entertainment 24
Sports 26
Brain Teasers 28

For More Information 30
Glossary 31
Index 32

4 AMERICAN STATES

INTRODUCTION

Millions of people know Florida as a great place to vacation, but it is much more than that. The long **peninsula**, with the Atlantic Ocean on one side and the Gulf of Mexico on the other, stretches hundreds of miles from Pensacola to Key West. This southeastern state produces the most **citrus** crops of any state in the United States. It also manufactures forest products, fruits and vegetables, dairy products, and beef. During winter months, Florida produces fruit and vegetable crops. These foods, along with Florida's famous orange juice, end up in homes across the United States and in other countries.

QUICK FACTS

Key West is the most southerly city in mainland United States.

Spain sold the land that is now Florida to the U.S. in 1819.

In 1861, Floridians developed a flag for their state. It included stars, stripes, and the motto "The Rights of the South at all Hazards!"

Florida's state song, "The Swanee River (Old Folks at Home)," was written in 1851. The Suwannee River flows from Georgia, through Florida, to the Gulf of Mexico.

Moonstone was adopted as Florida's state gem after American astronauts landed on the moon in 1969. It is not found in Florida, and astronauts did not find it on the moon.

Florida is best known for its delicious orange juice.

INTRODUCTION

Getting There

For most Americans, a trip to Florida means heading south, perhaps for thousands of miles. Florida is the most southerly state in the country. It is the closest state to South America. Georgia and Alabama border Florida to the north, and water surrounds most of the rest of the state.

Florida is 447 miles long, from the St. Marys River in the north to the tip of the Florida Keys. It is 361 miles wide, from the Atlantic Ocean on the east to the Perdido River on the west.

QUICK FACTS

Tallahassee, the capital city, was chosen in 1824 because it was halfway between St. Augustine and Pensacola. The new location meant the government no longer had to make the twenty-day trip by horse between St. Augustine and Pensacola for alternating sessions.

Florida's state flag includes a red diagonal cross with the state seal in the middle. The first settlers of Florida are represented on the seal, as are flowers, palm trees, rivers, lakes, and the motto "In God We Trust."

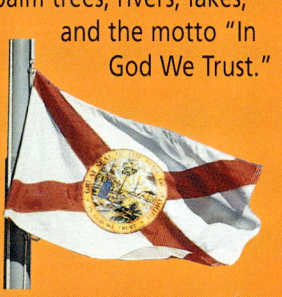

Location Map

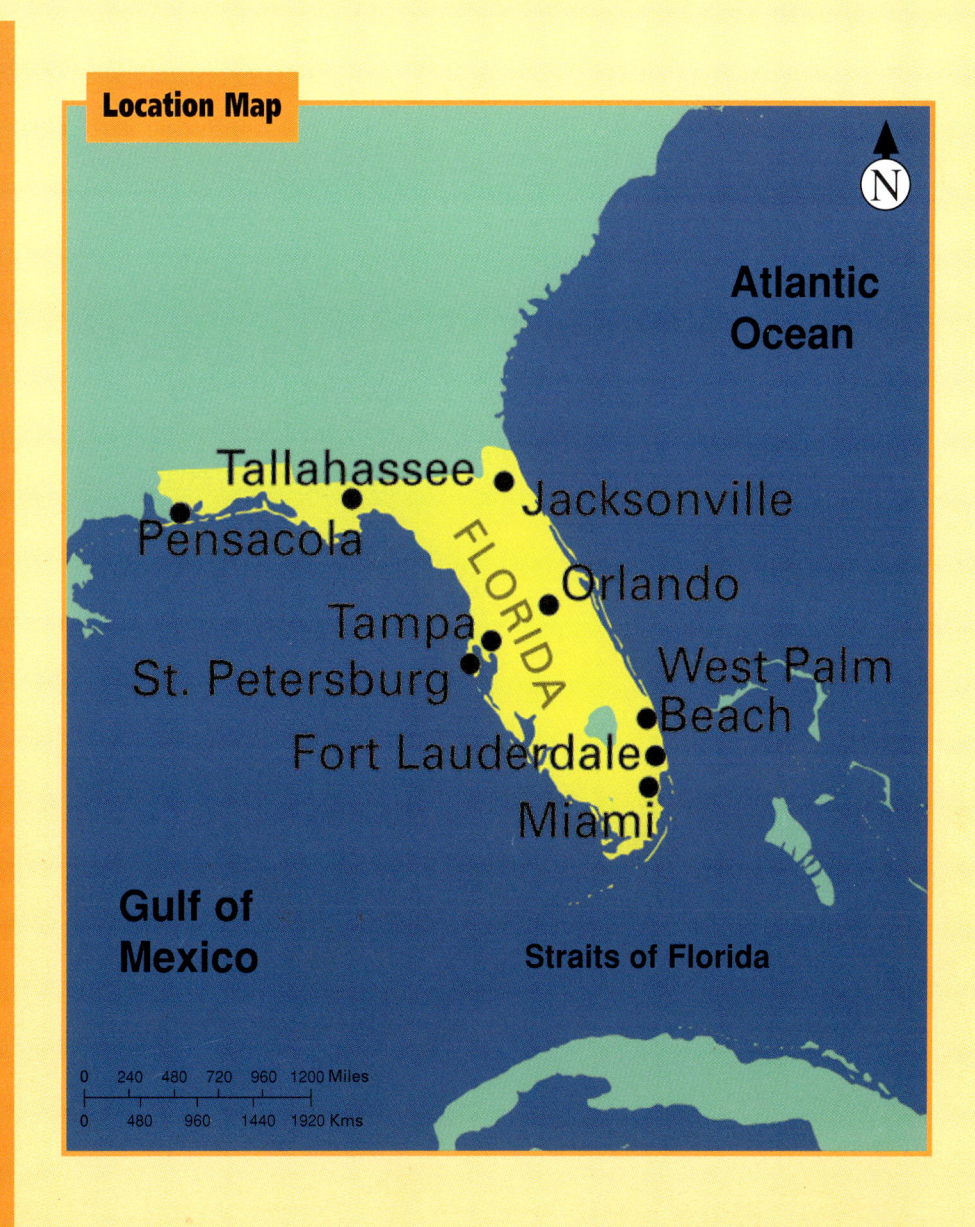

6 American States

The great climate attracts many tourists. It also attracts people who want to stay year round. Florida is one of the fastest growing states in the U.S. and the fourth most populated in the country. Dade County, which includes Miami, Hialeah, and Miami Beach, is the largest of the sixty-seven counties in Florida.

Along with the climate, water plays a huge role in drawing people to Florida. Natural springs gush with fresh water. There are more than 7,700 lakes in the state, and **wetlands** such as the Everglades and Big Cypress Swamp, cover large areas.

Ichetucknee Springs is one of many fresh water springs in Florida.

Quick Facts

Florida became a popular resort area more than one hundred years ago. People from the northern states discovered Florida's natural beauty and mild climate.

The state was prosperous until the **Great Depression** hit in the 1930s. The economy picked up again after World War II.

Some Florida Seminole Native Americans live on the Big Cypress reservation in the Everglades.

Introduction 7

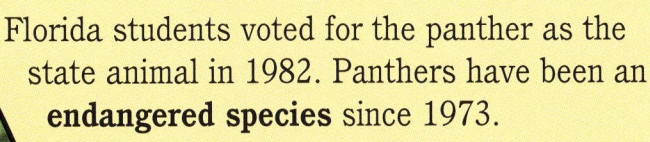

Florida students voted for the panther as the state animal in 1982. Panthers have been an **endangered species** since 1973. They are rarely seen anymore.

Florida's state marine mammal is the manatee. It is a gentle, walrus-like animal that can grow to more than 12 feet long and weigh up to 1,200 pounds. From a distance, the manatee's two front flippers look like hands. Manatee's flippers are used to hold their food and to steer when they are swimming.

The Florida panther is smaller than most Western cougars and has a shorter coat, longer legs, and smaller feet.

The manatee is known for its gentle nature and whiskered face.

Quick Facts

The panther is a large, long-tailed cat. It lives in forests and the Everglades, much the same as white-tailed deer. The deer are one of the cat's main foods.

Humans are responsible for much of the manatee's destruction. This endangered species frequently dies as a result of collisions with boats, pollution, and getting caught in fishing lines.

Florida also has a state reptile in the alligator, a state fish in the largemouth bass, and a state shell in the conch.

AMERICAN STATES

LAND AND CLIMATE

Until 400 million years ago, water separated Florida's north and south. Over millions of years, layers of sand and **fossilized** shell have built up in the water, creating flat, marshy land. Humans have also changed the landscape by draining marshes, filling in bays, and cutting down forests.

The Atlantic Coastal Plain includes coral reefs and wetlands on the mainland. The hilly areas of the Florida Uplands house much of the state's farming. The Everglades and Big Cypress Swamp are found in the Gulf Coastal Plain.

Florida's southern location gives it long, hot summers and short, mild winters. Heavy rainfall often occurs between April and November. Hurricane season lasts from late June to early November.

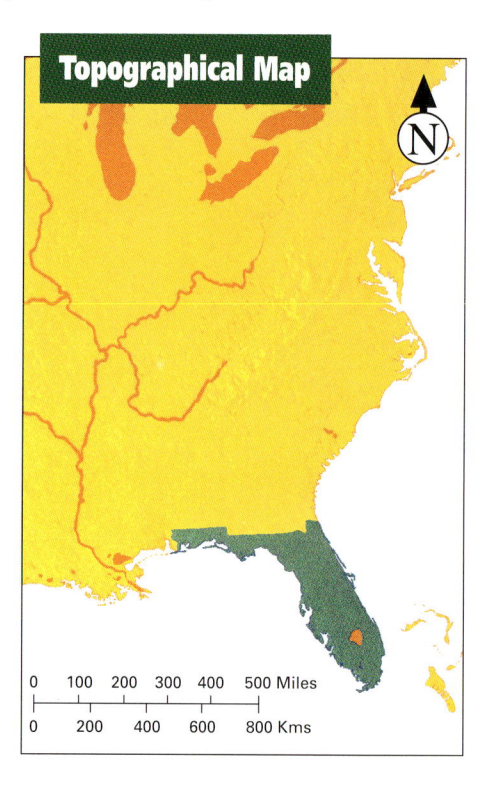

Quick Facts

No matter where you are in Florida, you are never more than 60 miles from a beach.

Florida has the longest coastline of any state except Alaska: 2,276 miles.

The average summer temperature is 80.5° F in the north and 82.7° F in the south. Average winter temperatures range from 53° F to 68.5° F.

Florida is made up of three land regions: the Atlantic Coastal Plain on the east, the Florida Uplands in north and central Florida, and the Gulf Coastal Plain in the west.

The hottest day ever recorded in Florida was June 29, 1931, when the temperature rose to 109° F in Monticello. The coldest temperature recorded was –2° F in Tallahassee in 1899.

Topographical Map

Corals are tiny animals related to jellyfish.

GEOGRAPHY

QUICK FACTS

More than 4 billion trees have been planted in Florida since 1928.

Farming used to be a main source of income. Today, fewer than 3 percent of people farm for a living.

Sunshine is an important resource in Florida. With about 220 days of sunshine per year, Florida lives up to its nickname as "the Sunshine State."

Florida is the leading state in the country in the production of phosphate. Phosphate is important to farmers, as it is used to make fertilizer.

NATURAL RESOURCES

Florida has an important **phosphate** mining industry. Deposits are usually found 15 to 30 feet below the earth's surface. Early miners used picks and shovels to mine phosphate. Electricity and machines have made mining easier, allowing workers to mine large areas. Thousands of acres are now mined, producing millions of tons of phosphate.

Trees are another important natural resource. The state has more than 15.7 million acres of forest grown for lumber. Pine is the main **commercial** tree. It is used to make paper and other related products. Most tree farming happens in north Florida, but some forest land is found in the southwestern region of the state.

Fish and other marine animals are another major resource. Florida ranks high in the country for the amount of seafood it produces. Commercial fishers sell their catches to restaurants and factories.

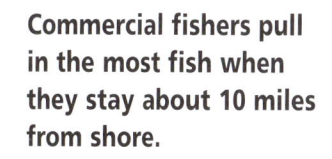

Commercial fishers pull in the most fish when they stay about 10 miles from shore.

A typical phosphate mine in Florida produces 10,000 tons of phosphate rock per acre.

10 American States

PLANTS AND ANIMALS

Florida's heat and unique environment make it home to plants and animals that are not found anywhere else in the country. Alligators and crocodiles are likely the best known animals in the state. However, a wide variety of living things, from tiny dragonflies to giant sea turtles, live there. Flamingos, ibises, and herons wade in warm, marshy areas along the coast. Warm temperatures also attract thousands of **migratory** birds that fly south for the winter.

Colorful plants such as orchids, lilies, and purple morning glories grow in different **habitats**. Mangrove trees grow well in warm, salty water along the coast. Cypress trees also live in wet areas. Forests of pine, beech, and magnolia trees cover almost half of the state and are home to deer, foxes, and wildcats, including the panther.

Quick Facts

The largest alligator ever recorded in Florida was 17 feet, 5 inches long.

Citrus trees are native to the Far East, such as China. They have been grown in Florida for more than 400 years.

Flamingos are pink because of natural chemicals in the shrimp and other foods they eat.

Fish, shellfish, birds, and other wildlife feed and raise their young among the roots of mangrove trees.

The cypress tree is the most flood-tolerant of all trees in Florida.

The crocodile uses its enormous snout to attack prey and predators.

GEOGRAPHY

QUICK FACTS

Sea turtles may travel hundreds or thousands of miles to feed and nest. These animals can live up to sixty years.

More than eighty kinds of land animals and 400 kinds of birds live in Florida. Almost 4,000 different kinds of plants grow in the state.

The Everglades and Big Cypress Swamp are huge wetland areas in southwest Florida where thousands of animals, plants, and birds live. The Everglades are the only place in the world where alligators and crocodiles live side by side. Two dozen kinds of snakes, only four of them poisonous, live in the Everglades, too. Colorful insects, including the lubber grasshopper and the sulphur butterfly, are also found there.

Catfish, marlins, sailfish, and sharks swim in the waters off the coast of Florida. So do many kinds of sea turtles, from small ridleys to giant leatherbacks. Crabs, clams, crayfish, and oysters live in salt water close to the coast. Largemouth bass, the state's official freshwater fish, grow larger in Florida than they do in other parts of the country. Sometimes these huge fish can weigh up to 20 pounds.

A giant sulphur butterfly can be as big as a child's hand.

Largemouth bass prefer to swim in areas that contain logs, debris, and weeds.

AMERICAN STATES

TOURISM

Beaches and hot weather draw millions of tourists to Florida each year. Some people want to escape the cold at home, while others come for the amusement parks, fishing, and the many natural areas that Florida offers.

Walt Disney World is the most famous tourist attraction in Florida and one of the biggest attractions in the world. Other parks in and around Orlando invite visitors to experience the magic of Hollywood filmmaking or watch dolphins and killer whales play in the water.

More than 1 million people visit Everglades National Park every year. The park is the largest remaining **subtropical** wilderness in the continental United States. Within its 1,506,539 acres are fresh and salt water areas, tropical hardwood forests, offshore coral reefs, and a wide variety of plants and animals.

QUICK FACTS

The area around Orlando and Osceola has more hotel rooms than New York City.

About 100,000 people work in amusement centers in Florida, and 18,000 people work in car rental outlets.

Visitors to Florida can learn about space at the Kennedy Space Center.

Before he died in 1966, Walt Disney bought 28,000 acres of land near Orlando to build Walt Disney World. The giant amusement park opened on October 1, 1971.

Dolphins are known for their grace, intelligence, playfulness, and friendliness.

Clearwater Beach is one of many beaches that Floridians enjoy.

Economy

QUICK FACTS

Cape Canaveral, where rockets, missiles, and space shuttles are tested and launched, is also the site of several science research companies.

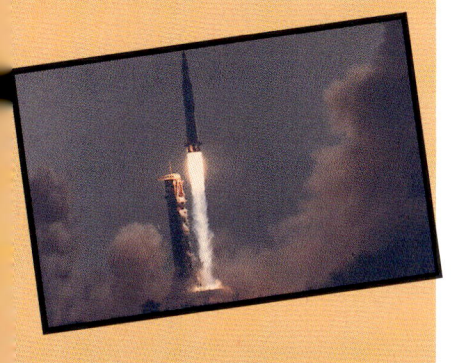

The first railroad in Florida ran 22 miles from Tallahassee to Port Leon on St. Mark's Bay. It was completed in 1838.

The first space mission to the moon lifted off from the Kennedy Space Center on July 16, 1969.

More than 40 million people visit Florida every year. Popular tourist spots are Miami Beach, Daytona Beach, Tampa Bay, and St. Petersburg. The Orlando area contributes the most to the tourism industry.

INDUSTRY

Tourism has always been an important industry in Florida. In the 1870s, businessmen such as Henry Flagler and Henry B. Plant began building railroads to link Florida to the north. They also built hotels close to their railroad lines to accommodate tourists.

Tourism is now the largest industry in Florida. It has created the need for smaller industries, such as wine-making and gardening.

Farming is another important industry. It does not employ huge numbers of people, but Florida produces fruits and vegetables, as well as most of the nation's orange and citrus crops. Many of these crops are **processed,** or made into other products.

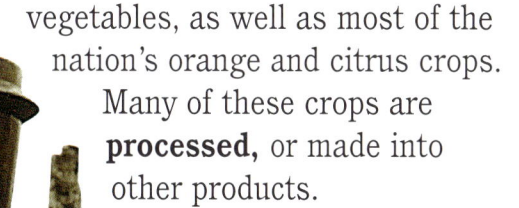

Florida's rail system has been running since 1838.

14 American States

QUICK FACTS

The Tropicana factory in Bradenton has sent 250,000 quarts of orange juice to Los Angeles, California, in one year.

Most Florida orange trees bloom in March and April.

Almost all Florida oranges are picked by hand, but some farmers use mechanical harvesters. One of these harvesters is called a trunk shaker. It clamps onto the tree and shakes the fruit loose.

Florida's fishing industry supplies enough seafood every year for more than 200 million seafood dinners.

GOODS AND SERVICES

Most people would have no trouble naming one of the most important goods produced in Florida. Oranges are probably the first thing people think of. Whether oranges are fresh, squeezed into juice, or made into other products, they provide a huge source of income for Florida farmers.

Other citrus crops in Florida include grapefruit, lemons, limes, and tangerines. To get an idea of how much citrus fruit grows in Florida, consider this: During the 1998–1999 growing season, Florida farmers picked 243 million boxes of fruit, down from a record of 304 million boxes the year before. Harvest season may start as early as August for some kinds of fruit, and it continues until June.

Oranges are critical crops in Florida. Eighty percent of the state's oranges are consumed as juice.

Economy   15

During the winter, when other parts of the country cannot grow food because of cold weather, Florida workers harvest tomatoes, potatoes, celery, carrots, lettuce, and other crops. Some farmers raise thoroughbred horses; others raise beef or dairy cattle, chickens, or hogs. Some people make their living by fishing for crab, lobster, or shrimp.

Many species of fish and shellfish live off Florida's coast.

Most people in Florida work in service jobs, which means they help other people and businesses. Service workers include people who work in amusement parks, stores, and other tourist attractions. Health-care workers, park rangers, politicians, and members of the army all provide services as well.

Many of the state's residents work in the service industry. This includes hotels, shopping malls, and restaurants.

Quick Facts

During the American Civil War, Florida supplied beef, pork, corn, molasses, and salt to feed soldiers in the southern armies.

Florida fruit is often shipped straight to other states and countries, such as Canada and Japan.

Florida grows almost 80 percent of all citrus crops in the United States.

Florida has the most seafood processing plants of any state in America.

16 American States

FIRST NATIONS

Native Americans were the first people to live in Florida. Scientists say they came to Florida about 12,000 years ago. They were **nomadic** hunters, which means they followed the animals they hunted and did not live in permanent settlements. They hunted with stone-tipped arrows and spears. Over hundreds of years, Florida's Native peoples changed their way of life. They started to live in villages, fish during winter months, and grow crops, such as corn. At least four major tribes lived in Florida, including the Calusa, Tequesta, Timucua, and Apalachee. Seminole Natives came from farther north.

By the early 1800s, white settlers wanted to take over the Native people's land and move Native Americans west of the Mississippi River. This led to the Seminole Wars. Many people died in the wars, and thousands of Native Americans were sent to live outside Florida. The descendants of the Native peoples who survived in Florida are members of today's Seminole tribe and Miccosukee tribe. Both of these native groups have succeeded in keeping their language and culture alive.

Quick Facts

The three Seminole Wars were fought between 1814 and 1858. By the late 1800s, Natives and white settlers had begun to trade peacefully.

Osceola led the Native warriors and fought to remain in Florida when they were being sent west. In 1837, he was captured by American troops. He died in prison several months later.

The Seminoles of Florida call themselves the "Unconquered People." They are descended from just 300 Natives who avoided capture by American troops in the 1800s.

In the Seminole Wars, British soldiers burned Native-American villages.

THE PAST

EXPLORERS

Close to Easter in 1513, Juan Ponce de Leon sailed to the northeast coast of Florida. The Spanish explorer landed near what is now St. Augustine and declared the land *Pascua Florida*, which means "feast of flowers" in Spanish.

Other Spanish explorers eager to find gold and glory in Florida followed Ponce de Leon. Panfilo de Narvaez and Cabeza de Vaca sailed there in 1527. They believed they would find rich Native villages to the north. They were disappointed to find only farming villages.

Other explorers, including Hernando de Soto and Tristan de Luna, sailed to Florida from Cuba and Mexico in the 1500s. None of them succeeded in setting up a permanent colony. In 1565, Pedro Menendez de Aviles built the first Spanish settlement in Florida in St. Augustine.

Quick Facts

Spanish explorers sailed to Florida hoping to find the same riches they had discovered in Mexico.

French explorers established Fort Caroline, near what is now Jacksonville, in 1564.

Ponce de Leon returned to Florida in 1521 to set up a permanent colony between Charlotte Harbor and Estero Bay in southwest Florida.

Hernando de Soto arrived on the west coast of Florida in search of gold and silver.

The Castillo de San Marcos is the oldest European fort in the United States.

18 American States

Quick Facts

By the early 1700s, only two dozen priests and about 400 Natives who had become Catholics lived in Florida.

During the 1600s, some Florida Native peoples lived in missions built by the Spanish. They adopted Catholic beliefs and prayed in Latin. They also kept some of their own traditions, such as building houses out of poles and grass and making stone points for their arrows.

Father Luis Cancer was the first priest to come to Florida. He was killed by Natives shortly after he arrived from Mexico in 1549.

MISSIONARIES

Explorers in search of riches were not the only people to sail to Florida in the 1500s. **Missionaries** who wanted to bring their message to the Native peoples of Florida also arrived in the area. These early Spanish Catholic priests did not always find the Native peoples welcoming or friendly. Also, the small number of priests found it hard to do missionary work in such a large area. British troops were always a threat. They attacked and destroyed Catholic missions, and Spain could not rebuild them.

Catholic missions were built by early settlers and missionaries.

THE PAST

QUICK FACTS

Early settlers thought the Everglade area was useless ground. In the early 1900s, they drained the area to make more farmland.

By the 1840s, steamboats ran on rivers such as the Apalachicola and the St. Johns, and Florida railroads were being planned.

In 1840, the population of Florida was more than 54,000, and almost half of these people were African-American slaves.

The British took control of Florida in 1763 and split it into two parts. St. Augustine was the capital of East Florida, and Pensacola was the capital of West Florida.

EARLY SETTLERS

In the early 1800s, Florida was mostly wilderness, with a few settlements of Native Americans, African Americans, and Spaniards. Many people raised cattle or grew crops. Some white settlers ran **plantations** where they relied on slave labor to grow and harvest crops. Poorer settlers survived by growing and making everything they needed to survive.

People who lived in Florida's large cities often worked in the lumber and cotton industries or in government. Industries such as mining led to the development of a railway system. The railroad linked major cities in Florida and connected Florida with the rest of the country. This allowed more people to visit the state.

By the early 1900s, Florida was growing quickly. Families settled in areas where swamps had been drained to create farmland. Others bought land in dry areas where canals had been built to supply water.

Plantation owners led Florida in wealth and power, but the slave plantation workers were quite poor.

POPULATION

A warm climate, beautiful scenery, and endless outdoor recreation bring more people to the Sunshine State every year. People come from all over the United States and from many other countries to settle in Florida. Most of them live in large cities along the coasts, where they enjoy the weather and the recreational activities that Florida offers.

Many retired people live in Florida, giving the state a high number of older residents. In the 1990 **census**, the population consisted of 83 percent white people, 14 percent African Americans, and 3 percent of people from other races, such as Native Americans and Asians. More than 12 percent of Floridians are of Hispanic origin. These people come from Spanish-speaking countries including Cuba, El Salvador, Colombia, and Venezuela. In 1999, the population of Florida reached 15,111,244.

Scuba diving is a favorite activity in the Keys.

Quick Facts

Since the 1940s, Florida has been **booming**. Soldiers who had trained at military bases in Florida during World War II returned with their families after the war.

Most Floridians were born in the United States, but about one in ten people has come from other countries, including Great Britain, Germany, Canada, and Cuba.

More than 15 million people live in Florida. It is the fourth most populated state after California, Texas, and New York.

Culture 21

POLITICS AND GOVERNMENT

Florida became a territory in 1821 and the twenty-seventh state in the Union in 1845. Like other states in the American South, Florida supported slavery and did not agree with policies in the northern states that freed slaves. On January 10, 1861, Florida voted to **secede**, or withdraw from the Union, and join with ten other southern states that had done the same.

About 15,000 soldiers from Florida fought for the South during the American Civil War, which lasted from 1861 to 1865. A few thousand people fought for the North. The southern states lost the war, and Florida rejoined the Union in 1868.

Today, government in Florida centers around the state capital in Tallahassee. About 3,000 people work in Florida's Capitol Building year-round. Offices for the governor, lieutenant, and other government employees are located in that building.

Governor Jeb Bush began a campaign to preserve and protect Florida's natural environment.

Quick Facts

Florida's first government meetings in 1824 were held in three log cabins.

The Battle of Olustee, fought in Florida, was one of the bloodiest battles in the Civil War.

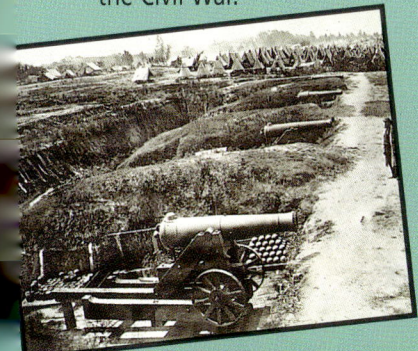

Florida's present Capitol Buildings opened in 1978. Builders used enough concrete in the Capitol to fill sixteen football fields, each one foot thick. The building rises 514 feet above sea level.

The Union flag resembled the British Union Jack flag.

CULTURAL GROUPS

People from at least six different cultural groups have made Florida what it is today: Native Americans, Spaniards, French, English, and, of course, Americans. Their traditions, foods, music, and beliefs continue to shape Florida's culture.

When white settlers first arrived from Spain, an estimated 350,000 Native peoples lived in what is now Florida. Many Native peoples were wiped out by war, disease, and the slave trade. Others were sent to live in states farther west. Today, about 2,000 Seminoles live on six reservations in the state. They proudly speak two languages, and they share their culture through their art, colorful clothing, and traditions such as basket weaving. Every spring, the Seminoles hold a Green Corn Dance—a spiritual event to give thanks. The gathering includes many hours of traditional "stomp dancing."

Quick Facts

The colorful patchwork clothing that many Seminoles wear is not based on traditional clothing. Seminoles adopted this style of dress in the 1920s.

Under the laws of slavery, African Americans were not allowed to keep African customs, speak African words, or practice African religion.

In 1980, more than 100,000 Cuban **refugees** came to the United States, most of them through Florida.

Seminole baskets are made of dried sweetgrass and held together with thread.

Because of its special importance, very few non-Native Americans may watch a traditional Green Corn Dance.

Culture

Quick Facts

Early settlers in St. Augustine held a Posey Dance every year. Based on a Spanish tradition, single girls attracted dates by placing a lit candle in their window.

The yellow, red, black, and white colors of the Miccosukee flag represent the circle of life: east, north, west, and south.

Miami's Little Havana was founded by Cubans between the late 1950s and early 1970s. Large groups of people from other Spanish-speaking countries, such as Nicaragua, Honduras, and Guatemala, now live in the area.

Close to 400 people from the Native tribe Miccosukees live in Florida today. They have kept their language, medicine, and traditional clans. Some Miccosukees live in **chickees**, which are homes made from thatched **palmetto** over a log frame. Like the Seminoles, they celebrate a Green Corn Dance every year.

Over the past 40 years, Hispanic people, many of them refugees from Cuba and Central America, have had a big influence on Florida culture. More than 2 million Hispanic people now call Florida home. They have brought with them their Spanish language, music, and foods, such as black beans, Cuban bread, and café con leche. Annual festivals, including the Cuban American Heritage Festival in Key West, celebrate Spanish culture. Miami and Hialeah both have large Hispanic populations. In some areas, billboards and signs are written only in Spanish. These areas are major centers for Central American banking, trade, and culture.

Some Miccosukee Native Americans wear traditional patchwork clothing.

People dance in the streets during the Cuban American Heritage Festival.

"Chickee" is the Seminole word for "house."

ARTS AND ENTERTAINMENT

QUICK FACTS

Actors and actresses who came from Florida include Faye Dunaway, Sidney Poitier, Burt Reynolds, and Ben Vereen.

Musicians Gloria Estefan, Little Richard, Tom Petty, and Jim Morrison were all born in Florida.

Writer Ernest Hemingway based many of his novels on his experiences in Florida, and the Florida Keys.

The name "Epcot Center" comes from Walt Disney's description of the park as an "experimental prototype community of tomorrow."

What do *Tarzan* and the *Creature from the Black Lagoon* have in common? Both films were shot in Florida. Florida's film industry has been strong for more than one hundred years. The climate and variety of natural areas in the state attracted early filmmakers looking for jungle settings or mysterious tropical islands. In the early 1900s, Jacksonville was a kind of Hollywood East. It boasted more than thirty film studios and 1,000 actors and **extras**. The booming industry eventually moved most of its work to Hollywood, but new studios have recently replaced them. Universal, Disney, and MGM all opened studios in Florida. By 1995, the state ranked third in filmmaking in the country.

Walt Disney World has provided large-scale entertainment to both tourists and local people since 1971. The vast amusement park features music and shows. Visitors to the Disney-MGM Studios can get a behind-the-scenes look at television shows and filmmaking.

Local Florida boys were hired as extras for the film, *Tarzan*.

Culture

Besides filmmaking, Florida has a wealth of music and theater. The New World Symphony in Miami Beach trains some of the top classical musicians in the country. Hundreds of graduates have gone on to perform with professional orchestras and music groups. Florida has a number of orchestras, including the Florida Orchestra, the Philharmonic Orchestra of Florida, and the Jacksonville Symphony.

Florida's Hispanic residents have introduced other kinds of music, such as salsa and Latin jazz. This music is especially popular in south Florida, where many Cuban and Central American people live.

There is also no shortage of theater in Florida, from the Gainesville Community Playhouse, the oldest community theater in Florida, to the Coconut Grove Playhouse in one of Miami's oldest neighborhoods.

Quick Facts

Florida's Cypress Gardens is sometimes called the "water ski capital of the world." It has produced water ski shows for more than sixty years, setting dozens of water skiing world records during that time.

The Florida Folk Festival in White Springs is the oldest state folk festival in America. The celebration of folk traditions, which takes place every Memorial Day weekend, started in 1953.

Salsa bands perform traditional Latin music.

Jazz music plays a large part in the night life in Ybor, Florida.

26 AMERICAN STATES

SPORTS

Just about every professional sport is represented in Florida, often in more than one city. The Jacksonville Jaguars, Miami Dolphins, and Tampa Bay Buccaneers all play in the National Football League (NFL), while the Florida Marlins compete in Major League Baseball. The Miami Heat and the Orlando Magic are members of the National Basketball Association (NBA). Other Florida-based professional teams play hockey and soccer. Some of them, such as the Florida Panthers and the Tampa Bay Lightning of the National Hockey League (NHL), were only formed during the 1990s.

QUICK FACTS

Florida boasts about 1,145 golf courses. Palm Beach County, with 150 golf courses, has more than any other county in Florida.

What do the words mariners, marauders, mustangs, missiles, moons, sharks, and suns have in common? All of them were suggested as names for Miami's new American Football League team in 1965.

A water skier named Chuck Sligh set the first water ski jump record of 49 feet at Cypress Gardens in 1947. Today, water skiers can jump more than 200 feet.

In 1972, the Miami Dolphins were the first NFL team to have an undefeated season.

Jacksonville Jaguars have to be quick to avoid being tackled.

Culture 27

Eighteen Major League Baseball teams hold their annual spring training camps in Florida. They also play exhibition games in the state before the regular season starts in April.

Florida high schools and colleges compete in all kinds of sporting events throughout the year. Florida State University, the University of Florida in Gainesville, and the University of Miami all have strong football teams that have competed in play-off games.

Jai alai, pronounced "high lie," is a sport that started in Spain hundreds of years ago. It is popular in Florida, especially in Miami. The handball-like game is played with a hard rubber ball, called a pelota, on a three-walled court, called a fronton. Players throw the ball with a wicker basket, called a cesta, attached to one arm. The ball can travel at 150 miles per hour.

Quick Facts

The Orange Bowl is played in Miami. The University of Miami won the first Orange Bowl football game ever played in 1933.

Jai alai is the fastest ball game in the world. In 1979, a player threw the ball at a speed of 188 miles per hour. A hockey slap shot, by comparison, moves at about 120 miles per hour.

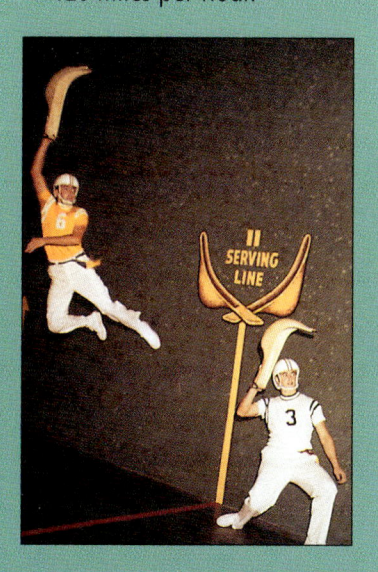

Florida is the leading state for greyhound racing, and its tracks make millions of dollars.

AMERICAN STATES

Brain Teasers

2 What is the longest river in Florida?

Answer: St. Johns River, 273 miles

1 What am I?

I am a big, pale brown cat with a long tail. People rarely see me, but I live in the forests of Florida and hunt deer. What am I?

Answer: Florida panther

3 What am I?

I love to prowl through lakes, swamps, and canals and sun myself on warm logs or sunny banks. I may grow up to 15 feet in length, but I am usually smaller than another Florida animal I resemble. What am I?

Answer: Alligator

4 Eye Spy

Which wading bird has eyes that point downward so it can spot fish more easily?

Answer: Great blue heron

ACTIVITIES

5
Approximately how many islands bigger than 10 acres are found in Florida?

Answer: More than 4,500.

7
Which two fruits are crossed to make Florida tangelos?

a. orange and tangerine
b. grapefruit and tangerine
c. grapefruit and orange
d. two different kinds of oranges

Answer: b) grapefruit and tangerine.

6
MAKE A GUESS

How many boxes of citrus fruit did farmers in Florida pick during the 1998–1999 season?

a. 1,000
b. 12,000
c. 347,000
d. 243 million

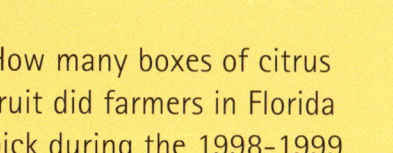

Answer: d) 243 million.

8
Moonwalking
Who was the first astronaut to walk on the moon following the launch of *Apollo 11* from Cape Canaveral?

Answer: Neil Armstrong

FOR MORE INFORMATION

Books

Aylesworth, Thomas G., and Virginia L. Aylesworth. *The South: Alabama, Florida, Mississippi.* New York: Chelsea House, 1996.

Morgan, Cheryl Koenig. *The Everglades.* Mahwah, NJ: Troll Associates, 1990.

Sirvaitis, Karen. *Florida.* Minneapolis, MN: Lerner Publications Company, 1994.

Web sites

There are many great web sites on the Internet about Florida. Here are a few you can look at to find out more about this fascinating state.

Everglades National Park
www.nps.gov/ever/

Florida History Internet Center
www.floridahistory.org/

The Seminole Tribe of Florida
www.seminoletribe.com

50 States — Florida
www.50states.com/florida.htm

The Ultimate Citrus Page
www.ultimatecitrus.com

Some web sites stay current longer than others. To find more Florida web sites, use your Internet search engines to look up such topics as "Florida," "Everglades," "Disney World," "Spring training," or any other topic you want to research.

GLOSSARY

booming: growing and prospering

census: the official counting of a population with details about such things as the individual's age, gender, and occupation

chickee: a log-frame home with a thatch roof, traditionally used by Seminoles and Miccosukees

citrus: trees or fruits from trees including lemon, lime, orange, and grapefruit

commercial: related to business; something done to earn money

endangered species: a group of plants and animals in danger of dying out

extras: people hired, often for the day, to appear in the background of a film

fossilized: the remains of ancient plants and animals hardened in rock

Great Depression: a time of poverty, unemployment, and drought that lasted from 1929 to 1934

habitats: the places where animals or plants are known to live or grow

migratory: birds that change the place where they live depending on the season

missionaries: people who travel to a foreign country to teach religion

nomadic: moving from place to place in search of somewhere to hunt or grow food

palmetto: palms with fan-shaped leaves

peninsula: a piece of land jutting out into a body of water and almost entirely surrounded by water

phosphate: a deposit formed over millions of years by layers of fossilized bones and shells. Phosphate is used to make fertilizer.

plantations: large estates or farms where crops were grown and harvested, usually by slaves

processed: treated to prevent decay or to create other products

refugees: people who flee to a foreign country because they fear for their safety

secede: to withdraw from membership of a group or country

subtropical: nearly tropical, which is very hot and humid

wetlands: areas of land that are wet or swampy

INDEX

alligators 7, 10, 11, 28

Big Cypress Swamp 6, 8, 11

Cape Canaveral 13, 29
Catholic 18
cattle 15, 19
citrus 4, 10, 13, 14, 15, 29, 30
crocodiles 10, 11
Cuba 17, 20, 22, 23, 25

de Leon, Ponce 17

Everglades 6, 7, 8, 11, 12, 19, 30

farming 8, 9, 13, 17
filmmaking 12, 24, 25
fishing 7, 12, 14, 15
flamingos 10
Florida Keys 5, 24
Florida Marlins 26
forests 4, 7, 8, 9, 10, 12, 28

Great Depression 6, 31
Green Corn Dance 22, 23
Gulf of Mexico 4

habitats 10, 31
Hialeah 6, 23
Hollywood 12, 24

jai alai 27

Kennedy Space Center 12, 13

largemouth bass 7, 11

manatee 7
marsh 8, 10
Mexico 17, 18
Miami Dolphins 26
Miccosukee 16, 23
mining 9, 19
missions 18

orange juice 4, 14
oranges 4, 13, 14, 29
orchestras 25
Orlando Magic 26
oysters 11

panther 7, 10, 28
peninsula 4, 31
Pensacola 4, 5, 19
phosphate 9, 31
pine 9, 10
plantations 19, 31

railroad 13, 19
reservations 6, 22

sea turtles 10, 11
Seminole 6, 16, 22, 23, 30
service 15
slaves 19, 21, 22
Spain 4, 18, 22, 27
St. Augustine 5, 17, 23
stomp dancing 22

Tallahassee 5, 8, 13, 21

Walt Disney World 12, 24
war 6, 15, 16, 20, 21, 22
wetlands 6, 8, 11, 31
white-tailed deer 7